Practice to [Learn]

FIRST GRADE ACTIVITIES

Editor in Chief/Project Director: Karen J. Goldfluss, M.S. Ed.

Editor: Eric Migliaccio

Co-Authors: Karen McRae, Eric Migliaccio

Imaging: James Edward Grace

Cover and Interior Design: Sarah Kim

Art Coordinator: Renee Mc Elwee

Creative Director: Sarah M. Fournier

Publisher: Mary D. Smith, M.S. Ed.

Teacher Created Resources
12621 Western Avenue
Garden Grove, CA 92841
Printed in U.S.A.

www.teachercreated.com
ISBN: 978-1-4206-8223-6
©2019 Teacher Created Resources
Made in U.S.A.

1

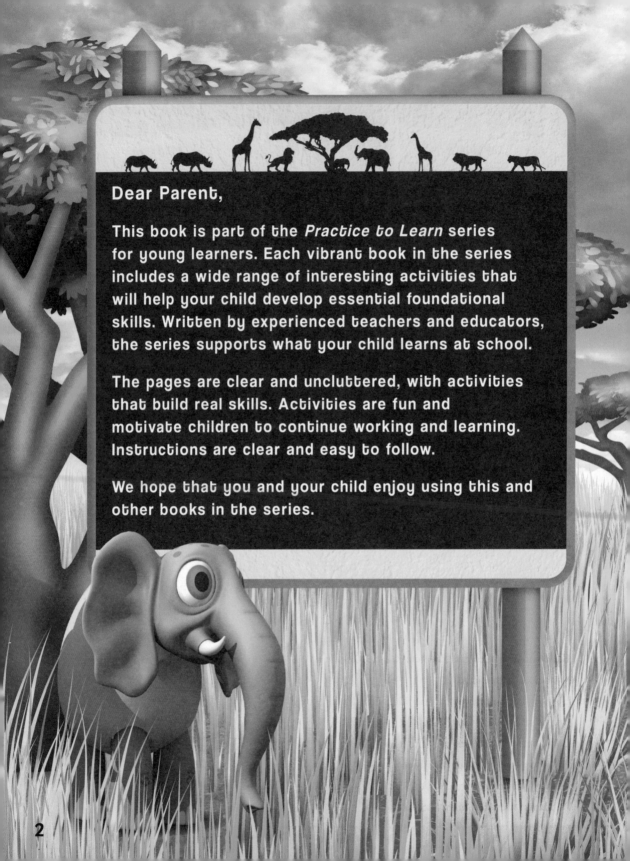

Dear Parent,

This book is part of the *Practice to Learn* series for young learners. Each vibrant book in the series includes a wide range of interesting activities that will help your child develop essential foundational skills. Written by experienced teachers and educators, the series supports what your child learns at school.

The pages are clear and uncluttered, with activities that build real skills. Activities are fun and motivate children to continue working and learning. Instructions are clear and easy to follow.

We hope that you and your child enjoy using this and other books in the series.

Contents

What to Expect

First grade is a whole new level in more ways than one! The academic rigor alone is far beyond what your child experienced in kindergarten. As children progress through first grade and toward second grade, they will most likely be expected to complete the following tasks in the following curriculum areas:

Reading

- Read level-appropriate books on their own with accuracy and understanding.
- Read high-frequency words.
- Remember the sequence of events in stories and retell them.

Writing

- Sound out words they hear and spell them based on those sounds.
- Write paragraphs with a topic sentence, supporting details, and a closing sentence.
- Print all letters legibly.

Math

- Count and write numbers up to 120.
- Count by 2s, 5s, and 10s up to 100.
- Add and subtract to 20.
- Tell time to the half hour.

Science

- Use tools like a ruler, scale, and magnifying glass.
- Conduct hands-on experiments.

Social Studies

- Locate one's country, the continents, and the oceans on a map.
- Make and use simple maps.

Around the Home

Keep learning fun and interesting with these games and activities:

▸ ## Reading: Sight Word Target Practice

Materials Needed: paper plates, a marker, painter's or masking tape, list of words, something soft (like a stuffed animal or soft ball) to throw in the house

On paper plates, write sight words that your child is learning (one word per plate). Find an open wall space and tape the plates to the wall. Once things are set up, you call out a word and your child tries to hit the correct plate with the soft object.

▸ ## Writing: Taste Test

Conduct a taste test with a writing twist! Choose a few foods that your child has never tasted before. Record the experience in writing.

Before tasting: Have your child draw a picture of the new food and write a sentence about its look and/or smell.

After tasting: Have your child write 2–3 sentences that describe the taste and texture of the food and the experience of eating it.

▸ ## Math: Buildable Bingo

Materials: paper, markers, pair of dice, stackable blocks

Creat a bingo board and write a number from 2–12 in each space. (It's ok to have duplicates.) Then, roll the dice and count/stack that amount of blocks. Put the finished stack on the correct number on the paper. When all the numbers on the paper have been covered, your child must count **all** the stacks of blocks to see how many there are **in all**.

▸ ## Social Studies: Following Cardinal Directions

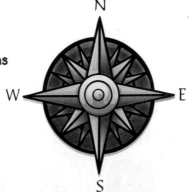

Ask your child to hide a treasure and then use cardinal directions to guide you to the right place. Your child can write out instructions, such as "Start at the door and take 3 medium steps north. Turn towards the couch and take 2 small steps east."

Short Matching

Draw a line to match each picture to its short vowel sound. Each sound should match two different pictures.

          short **a**

          short **e**

          short **i**

          short **o**

          short **u**

Say the name of the **number** you see below. Which short vowel do you hear? Color your answer.

    a   e   i   o   u

Long Matching

Draw a line to match each picture to its long vowel sound. Each sound should match two different pictures.

long **a**

long **e**

long **i**

long **o**

long **u**

Say the name of the **color** you see below. Which long vowel do you hear? Color your answer.

| a | e | i | o | u |

In the Beginning

Circle the two pictures in each row that begin with the same sound. Write the sound. Choose from the sounds in the box.

Sounds Box	cl	dr	pl	sh	st

	Circle two.			Write the sound.
Row 1				
Row 2				
Row 3				
Row 4				

At the End

Circle the two pictures in each row that end with the same sound. Write the sound. Choose from the sounds in the box.

Sounds Box	ck	ll	nk	nt	sh

	Circle two.	Write the sound.
Row 1		
Row 2		
Row 3		
Row 4		

Syllable Sort

How many syllables does each word have? Sort the words into the boxes below. For example, write the words with one syllable in the "1" box.

apple	banana	pear	kangaroo
kitten	shark	circle	square
triangle	butterfly	ant	spider

1

_____

_____

_____

_____

2

_____

_____

_____

_____

3

_____

_____

_____

_____

Draw a picture of a big animal with a long trunk.

Say the name of the animal you drew. How many syllables are in its name?

_____

Say the word for each picture. Write which vowel the r in the word controls? Choose from the answers in the box. The first answer is done for you.

Blend Box	ar	er	ir	or	ur

1.

ar
_____

2.

_____

3.

_____

4.

_____

5.

_____

6.

_____

7.

_____

8.

_____

9.

_____

Which Comes First?

Look at each set of words. Draw a picture of the word that comes first in alphabetical order.

Set 1

chicken   egg

Set 2

horse   car

Set 3

pineapple apple banana

Set 4

flower   garden   bug

Set 5

cake   coat   clock

Set 6

six   seven   start

Counting Cows

How many do you see in each row? Write the number
and the word. If there is more than one, add s or es to
make the word plural. The first one is done for you.

1.

      <u> 1 </u>   <u> COW </u>
        (number)   *(animal word)*

      <u> 2 </u>   <u> COWS </u>
        (number)   *(animal word)*

2.

      _____   _____
        (number)   *(animal word)*

      _____   _____
        (number)   *(animal word)*

3.

      _____   _____
        (number)   *(animal word)*

      _____   _____
        (number)   *(animal word)*

4.

      _____   _____
        (number)   *(animal word)*

      _____   _____
        (number)   *(animal word)*

5.

      _____   _____
        (number)   *(animal word)*

      _____   _____
        (number)   *(animal word)*

Out of Order

These sentences are out of order. Write them in order.

1. saw a We cat. black

   _____

   -

   _____

2. turtle slow. The was

   _____

   -

   _____

3. frog? that Is blue a

   _____

   -

   _____

4. new Her great! looks hat

   _____

   -

   _____

5. candles. cake had My six

   _____

   -

   _____

   -

   _____

Fix 'Em Up!

These sentences are missing some things! Can you fix them? Add capital letters and punctuation marks.

1. he and i ate candy

   _____

   -

   _____

2. are those shoes blue

   _____

   -

   _____

3. that cat is so fast

   _____

   -

   _____

4. will we fly on friday

   _____

   -

   _____

5. we swim a lot in july

   _____

   -

The Best Word

Look at the pictures. What is the best word to describe each one? Choose from the words in the box.

Answers	melting	metal	round
	smelly	sweet	warm

1. _____

2. _____

3. _____

4. _____

5. _____

6. _____

Rhyme Time!

Fill in the blank in each sentence. Choose a word that rhymes with the blue word in each sentence.

Answers	ants	bird	bug
	duck	frog	owl

1. I just saw a _____ going for a **jog**!

2. There is a _____ in my **truck**!

3. I am sure that _____ can't wear **pants**!

4. I will not **hug** that _____ on the **rug**!

5. I have heard a _____ say a **word**,

   but I've never heard an_____say a **vowel**!

Choose one of the sentences. Draw a picture of what it says.

A Tree Story

Read the story below. It is called "Three in a Tree." Underline all of the long e words that you read in the story. Answer the questions.

Three in a Tree

Dee and I see a tree. It has lots of green leaves. We see a brown nest in the tree. Are there any eggs? There are three! We watch but do not touch. We let the little birds be.

1. How many long e words did you underline in the story?

   _____

2. Which two colors do "Dee and I" see?

   _____

3. Which word from the story rhymes with much?

   _____

4. Which word from the story means more than one leaf?

   _____

5. Look at the story's title. What does the word three describe? Circle the correct answer.

   birds   eggs   leaves

Best Friends

Read the story below. Answer questions about the story.

This is a picture of me and my best
friend. My best friend's name is Rex.
Some say that we look like brothers.
Rex and I were not always friends. I did not like him
at first. He was big and smelly. He snored loudly. But
he was also nice. He shared his treats with me. He
barks at mean dogs. Mean dogs stay away. Rex is the
best! I don't care if he snores!

1. What kind of animal is Rex?_____

2. What kind of animal is telling the story?_____

3. Write three words that this animal uses to describe Rex.

_____

_____

4. Why might people think Rex and his friend look like
   brothers?

_____

_____

5. What part of the story helped you answer question #4?

_____

Finding Information

This page comes from a book about the five senses.

My Five Senses

Table of Contents

Use the above page to fill in the chart below.

		Name of Chapter	Page in Book
1.	Matt wants to know about how our ears take in sound. Where should he look in the book?		
2.	Ann wants to know how her tongue can tell that she is eating sweet food. Where should she look in the book?		
3.	Kel wants to know what happens when you grab a hot pan with your bare hand. Where should she look?		

4. Look at the picture on the page above. Where do you think you would find that picture in this book?

Chapter Name: _____ Page Number: _____

Picture This

Read the story. Draw a picture. Show what the story describes.

Read.

Mo sat under a large tree. Mo had a long tail, a long mane, and a long horn. The horn stuck out of the middle of her head. The tree had four apples that hung above Mo's head. She reached up to a low apple. She gently grabbed the apple between her teeth. Mo loved apples!

Draw.

All On the Line

Use the number line to help you solve the word problems.

0 1 2 3 4 5 6 7 8 9 10 11 12 13 14 15 16 17 18 19 20

1. Start on 14. Count forward 5. What number are you on?

   I am on ___. Show the math problem: ___ + ___ = ___

2. Start on 13. Count forward 4. What number are you on?

   I am on ___. Show the math problem: ___ + ___ = ___

3. Start on 9. Count forward 7. What number are you on?

   I am on ___. Show the math problem: ___ + ___ = ___

4. Start on 17. Count backward 6. What number are you on?

   I am on ___. Show the math problem: ___ − ___ = ___

5. Start on 11. Count backward 9. What number are you on?

   I am on ___. Show the math problem: ___ − ___ = ___

6. Start on 13. Count backward 7. What number are you on?

   I am on ___. Show the math problem: ___ − ___ = ___

Over and Under 100

Use the number line to help you solve the word problems.

```
 90  91  92  93  94  95  96  97  98  99 100 101 102 103 104 105 106 107 108 109 110
```

1. Start on 101. Count forward 9. What number are you on?

   I am on ___. Show the math problem: ___ + ___ = ___

2. Start on 103. Count backward 8. What number are you on?

   I am on ___. Show the math problem: ___ − ___ = ___

3. Start on 93. Count forward 8. What number are you on?

   I am on ___. Show the math problem: ___ + ___ = ___

4. Start on 107. Count backward 16. What number are you on?

   I am on ___. Show the math problem: ___ − ___ = ___

5. Start on 91. Count forward 10. What are you on?

   I am on ___. Show the math problem: ___ + ___ = ___

6. Start on 108. Count backward 12. What are you on?

   I am on ___. Show the math problem: ___ − ___ = ___

More or Less

Count the items. Write the number of each. Then write the > (greater than) or < (less than) symbol to show if the first group has more or less than the second group.

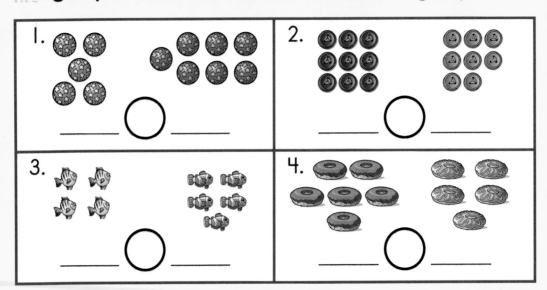

1. _____ ◯ _____

2. _____ ◯ _____

3. _____ ◯ _____

4. _____ ◯ _____

Write the correct symbol (>, <, or =) between the two numbers.

5. 13 ◯ 21	**6.** 30 ◯ 29	**7.** 52 ◯ 51
8. 62 ◯ 62	**9.** 79 ◯ 97	**10.** 81 ◯ 76

Odd or Even?

If the space has an even number, color it blue.
If the space has an odd number, color it red.

For some spaces, you must solve a math problem first!

Missing Numbers

Write the missing number that comes before the others.

1. _____, 35, 36

2. _____, 62, 63

3. _____, 81, 82

4. _____, 50, 51

Write the missing number that comes after the others.

5. 35, 36, _____

6. 18, 19, _____

7. 89, 90, _____

8. 68, 69, _____

Write the missing number that between the others.

9. 58, _____, 60

10. 29, _____, 31

11. 98, _____, 100

12. 110, _____, 112

Write the missing numbers that come before and after.

13. _____, 56, _____

14. _____, 72, _____

15. _____, 33, _____

16. _____, 99, _____

Color By Numbers

Solve each addition or subtraction problem.
- If the answer is **< 20**, color the space **red**.
- If the answer is **> 30**, color the space **blue**.
- If the answer is **from 20–30**, color the space **green**.

11 − 10	18 + 8
20 + 12	13 − 3
15 + 10	20 + 16
3 + 21	20 + 19
19 + 9	27 + 1
13 + 3	11 + 24
12 − 0	25 − 2
30 − 30	14 + 4
20 + 20	28 − 8
29 + 11	28 + 0
7 + 4	7 + 14
10 − 1	19 + 1
6 + 6	6 + 16
15 − 10	18 − 0
21 + 20	28 − 2
20 − 0	42 − 10
1 + 7	31 + 0
10 + 13	27 + 8

27

Skip Ahead

Fill in the blanks to count by 2s.	Fill in the blanks to count by 5s.	Fill in the blanks to count by 10s.

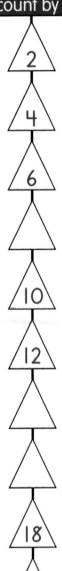

2
4
6

10
12

18

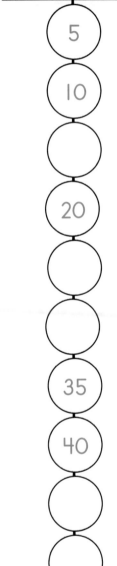

5
10

20

35
40

20
30

60

100

Add up how much each set of coins is worth.

Remember:

 = 1¢   = 5¢   = 10¢   = 25¢

1.

 +   =

2.

 + +   =

3.

 +   =

4.

 + + =

5.

 + + =

6.

 +  + +   =

Two Problems in One

Each of these word problems can be used to solve an addition and a subtraction problem. Solve them all!

 Theo's Thrift had a great week. They sold 13 hats, 7 belts, and 8 neckties.

1. How many more hats did they sell than belts? _____

2. How many items did they sell altogether? _____

 Lucky clovers have four leaves on them. Annie found seven lucky clovers. She gave one to each of her four sisters.

3. After giving each sister a clover, how many did Annie have left? _____

4. How many total leaves were there on the clovers Annie found? _____

 Coco's Cool Scoops sold 20 scoops of ice cream in one hour! Six scoops were chocolate, 8 scoops were vanilla, and 4 scoops were strawberry. The rest were mint chip.

5. How many vanilla and chocolate scoops did they sell combined? _____

6. How many mint chip scoops did the store sell? _____

A Colorful Graph

Students in Ms. Mack's class had a choice of four notebook colors. After they chose colors, the class made a graph. The graph shows how many students chose each color.

Color	1	2	3	4	5	6
blue	■	■	■	■	■	■
red	■	■	■	■	■	
green	■	■	■	■		
purple	■	■	■	■	■	

1. Which color did the least number of students choose?

_____

2. Which two colors did the same number of students choose?

_____

3. What is the name of the students' teacher?

_____

4. Fill in the math sentence below to show how many students there are altogether in the class?

_____ + _____ + _____ + _____ = _____

5. Show how many students chose each color. Use blue, red, and green markers or pencils to fill in the bubbles below. The purple bubbles have been filled in for you.

● ● ● ○ ○ ○ ○ ○ ○

● ● ○ ○ ○ ○ ○ ○ ○

Order the Story

Some stories need to be told in order. Look at the story parts. Rewrite them in order. Draw a picture for each part.

Story Parts	
When the cake was cool, we put icing on it.	We mixed it all up in a bowl.
Dad put the mix into the oven.	We got eggs, flour, and sugar.

Draw pictures here.

Rewrite the story in order here.

_____

_____

_____

_____

_____

_____

_____

_____

First to Last

Stories go in an order. Transition words help readers know this order. Here are some transition words.

First	Second	Third	Next
Then	Last	Finally	

Choose a word from the list to start each sentence below. Choose a different word each time.

School Mornings

_____, I wake up in the morning.

_____, I have toast and milk for breakfast.

_____, I brush my teeth and get dressed.

_____, Mom drives me to school.

_____, I play with Justin and Lily until the bell rings.

An Amazing Tale

Writers use words that describe the things in their stories. This helps readers "see" the story. Finish the story below. Add words that will help your reader "see" the story.

The giraffe at the zoo has a _____

neck. It uses its neck to eat leaves from the top of

a _____ tree. We hear a

_____ sound as the giraffe chews the

leaves. Next, we will visit a cage full of _____ lions.

I can't wait to see their _____teeth!

What happens next? Write two sentences about the lions' cage. Use at least one describing word in each sentence.

_____

_____

_____

_____

Then This Happened

Read the story. Then . . .

- Add to the story. Tell what happens next.
- Give the story a title.
- Draw a picture that shows some part of the story.

_____
(Write title here.)

Mrs. Froom stood in front of the room. A large box sat next to her desk. The box had holes all over and a rope around it. Mrs. Froom began to cut the rope. She said, "I can't wait to show you our new class pet.!" The rope fell down and one side of the box swung open. That was when we saw it!

_____

_____

_____

_____

_____

In My Opinion

Give your opinions. Explain your answers.

In your opinion . . .

What are two things that every good book should have in it?

1. _____

2. _____

Why? _____

_____

_____

_____

In your opinion . . .

Which season is the best? Circle one answer.

      fall   **winter**   spring   summer

Why? Give two reasons. _____

_____

_____

_____

Here's How It's Done

There are some things you do all the time. You just know how to do them. See if you can tell someone else how to do something. Write really clear instructions.

Name three things that you are really good at doing?

1. _____

2. _____

3. _____

Choose one thing from your list. Tell someone else how to do your thing in four simple steps.

How to _____

First _____

Next _____

Then _____

Finally _____

Dare to Compare

Some writing compares two things. These things are alike in some ways but different in others. Choose one of the pairs of things below. Put a check next to your choice. Compare the two things in writing.

- ☐ apples and oranges
- ☐ breakfast foods and dinner foods
- ☐ books and movies
- ☐ school days and summer days

Here is how these two things compare:

_____

_____

_____

_____

Circle one: I think these things are more   alike   different because

_____

_____

_____

_____

What are these characters thinking? Use clues from the pictures to guess what they might be thinking.

This bear is thinking . . .

_____

_____

_____

_____

_____

What clues did you use to guess this character's thoughts?

_____

_____

This knight is thinking . . .

_____

_____

_____

_____

_____

What clues did you use to guess this character's thoughts?

_____

_____

Living Things

The world is full of living things. Living things grow during their lives. People, animals, and insects are living. So are trees and plants.

In the picture below, can you find at least 7 living things? Circle them. Find at least 4 non-living things. Draw an X through them.

Oakview Park

Parents and Children

Some babies look a lot like their parents. Some do not. Look at the pictures below. Draw a line to match a baby on the left with its parent on the right.

1.    a.

2.   b.

3.   c.

4.   d.

5.   e.

Which babies look the **least** like their parents?

_____

Animal Types

Four of the most common types of animals are mammals, reptiles, amphibians, **and** invertebrates.

> ▸ **Mammals** have fur or hair and give birth to live young. Humans, apes, dogs, cats, cows, horses, pigs, and mice are mammals.

> ▸ **Reptiles** have scales and lay eggs. Snakes, lizards, crocodiles, and turtles are reptiles.

> ▸ **Amphibians** often begin life in water and then move to land. Frogs, newts, and salamanders are amphibians.

> ▸ **Invertebrates** do not have a backbone. Insects, spiders, worms, and snails are invertebrates.

Look at the name of each animal below.

- If the animal is a **mammal**, color the space **brown**.
- If the animal is a **reptile**, color the space **green**.
- If the animal is an **amphibian**, color the space **blue**.
- If the animal is an **invertebrate**, color the space orange.

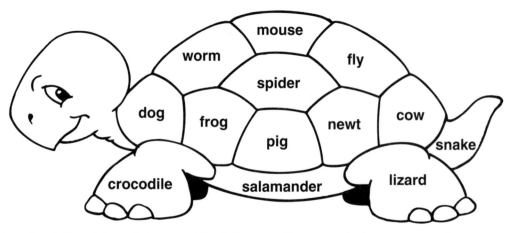

Look at the big picture. What **type** of animal do you see?

_____

Living things need the right place to live and grow. Read about three places.

- ▶ **Place A** is warm and a bit wet. It has lots of green plants and trees.
- ▶ **Place B** is very cold. It has a lot of ice and snow.
- ▶ **Place C** is very hot and dry. The land is mostly flat.

Now read about three animals. Which place would they like to live in? Color each correct answer.

1. tarantula

   (Color one.)

   A **tarantula** hunts at night.
   It lives in a hole in the ground.

   - Place A
   - Place B
   - Place C

2. toucan

   (Color one.)

   A **toucan** lives in a hole in a tree.
   It has short wings, and it can't fly far.

   - Place A
   - Place B
   - Place C

3. polar bear

   (Color one.)

   A **polar bear** has thick, white fur.
   It has a thick layer of fat under its fur.

   - Place A
   - Place B
   - Place C

Everybody Sleeps!

Sleep helps our minds and bodies work as best as they can. But not all people need the same amount of sleep. This chart shows about how much sleep each day that people of different ages need.

Use the chart to answer the questions.

Key: 🕐 = 2 hours 🕐 = 1 hour

newborn babies (0–2 months old)	🕐	🕐	🕐	🕐	🕐	🕐	🕐	🕐
infants (3–11 months old)	🕐	🕐	🕐	🕐	🕐	🕐	🕐	
toddlers (1–3 years old)	🕐	🕐	🕐	🕐	🕐	🕐		
preschoolers (3–5 years old)	🕐	🕐	🕐	🕐	🕐	🕐		
school-age children (5–11 years old)	🕐	🕐	🕐	🕐	🕐			
adolescents (11–17 years old)	🕐	🕐	🕐	🕐	🕐			
adults (over 18 years old)	🕐	🕐	🕐	🕐				

1. About how many hours of sleep you need? _____

2. About how many hours do adults need? _____

3. About how many fewer hours does an adult need than a newborn baby needs? Fill in the math problem you used to find the answer.

   _____ – _____ = _____ hours

4. Look at these two statements. Circle the one that is true.

   We need more sleep as we get older.

   We need more sleep when we are younger.

Everybody Blinks!

Blinking is important. It keeps our eyes clean and moist. Most people blink about 15 times per minute. Very young babies blink much less. Their eyes don't get as dry. Also, computer users tend to blink less. This can cause their eyes to get dried out.

Look at the graph. Use it to answer the questions below.

Minutes	1	2	3	4	5
Times Average Person Blinks	15	30	45	60	75
Times Young Baby Blinks	2	4	6	8	10
Times Computer User Blinks	7	14	21	28	35

1. How many times does the average person blink in 4 minutes? _____

2. A young baby blinks 10 times in 5 minutes. How many times would a baby blink in 10 minutes? _____

3. Who would blink most? Fill in the correct answer.

   Ⓐ a young baby in 10 minutes

   Ⓑ a computer user in 4 minutes

   Ⓒ the average person in 2 minutes

Matter is everything around us. Most of the matter that we see around us is either a solid or a liquid.

Liquids do not have a shape of their own. Solids do. An apple is solid. It can sit on a table and stay in its shape. But apple juice is a liquid. If you poured apple juice on a table, it would spill all over! A liquid needs to be inside a solid to keep its shape.

Look at each picture. Write solid on the line next to each solid. Write liquid on the line next to each liquid.

1. the glass ____solid____ the juice _____	2. the oil _____ the jar _____
3. the bowl _____ the water _____ the fish _____	Draw a picture of a liquid in a solid. Label each part.

Sunny Planets

There are 8 planets in our solar system. These 8 planets move around our very hot Sun. The planets that are closer to the Sun are warmer. The ones that are farther from the Sun are colder.

This diagram shows the Sun and the eight planets in order. Use this diagram to answer the questions below.

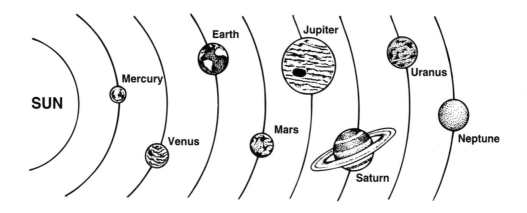

1. Mercury is the 1st planet from the Sun. Earth is the _____ planet from the Sun.

2. Which planet is 6th from the Sun? _____

3. Which planet is most likely the coldest? _____

   Why? _____

   _____

4. The largest planet in our solar system is 5th from the Sun. What is the name of the largest planet? _____

There are four seasons: winter, spring, summer, and fall. Which seasons do the pictures show? How do you know?

This picture shows the season of

_____

Here is how I know: _____

_____

This picture shows the season of

_____

Here is how I know: _____

_____

This picture shows the season of

_____

Here is how I know: _____

_____

This picture shows the season of

_____

Here is how I know: _____

_____

What's the Weather?

Weather scientists look at weather patterns and try to tell us what the weather will be like for the next week or two. The chart below shows a weather forecast. It gives the temperatures. Higher temperatures mean warmer weather. It shows a picture. This tells us if we can expect lots of sun, clouds, rain, wind, or snow.

Use this chart to answer the questions below.

Monday	Tuesday	Wednesday	Thursday	Friday
80 degrees	75 degrees	63 degrees	65 degrees	66 degrees

1. Which day should be the warmest? _____
2. Which day should be the coldest? _____
3. On which day should you carry an umbrella? _____
4. Which day should be the most windy? _____
5. How many degrees cooler will Tuesday be than Monday?

    Show your work here.   Answer

    _____ degrees cooler

6. How many degrees warmer will Tuesday be than Thursday?

    Show your work here.   Answer

    _____ degrees cooler

My Timeline

A timeline is a diagram. It has a date on one side and an event on the other. We use timelines to show when things happened in history. You can do the same to show when things happened in your history.

Fill out the timeline of your life. Add at least four events onto the timeline. Your events can be in words or in pictures. The first one has been started for you.

Age 6

Age 5

Age 4

Age 3

Age 2

Age 1

Birth

You were born!

Date: _____

City: _____

Time Changes

Events that happened long ago are in the **past**. Events that are happening now are in the **present**. Event that will happen years from now are in the **future**.

For each time period, draw a picture. Also, list a few things that you think of when you think of that time period. A few have been written in for you.

Past	Present	Future
horses used for transportation George Washington _____ _____ _____	smartphones Internet _____ _____ _____	_____ _____ _____ _____

The Big Four

When we move or travel, we go in a direction. There are four main directions. The compass to the right shows them.

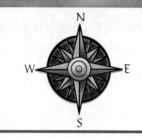

Answer the questions below about directions.

1. What are the four main directions? _____

_____   _____   _____

2. Which directions are opposite from each other?

____North____ is opposite from _____.

_____ is opposite from ____East____.

3. When we look at a map, north is toward the top of the map.

   a. Which direction is toward the bottom? _____

   b. Which direction is toward the right? _____

4. Look at this map.

Hill City

Park City   Sun City

Lake City

   a. Which city is to the north?

   _____

   b. Which city is to the west?

   _____

Getting Around

We use transportation to get from one place to another. Walking is a form of transportation. So are bikes, cars, buses, trains, planes, and anything else that helps us get around. Which form of transportation is the best? It depends on where you are going.

What would you use to get to the following places?

a. to school

_____

b. to your neighbor's house

_____

c. to another city

_____

d. to another country

_____

e. to an island

_____

f. to your local park

_____

Some forms of transportation carry a lot of people at once. If you want to get on one of these forms, you have to go to the place where the trip begins. Look at the pictures of places and transportation forms. Draw lines to match them.

airplane

train

cruise ship

port

airport

station

People Who Help

Look at the picture of people who help in our communities. Answer the questions below with the workers' names.

pharmacist

electrician

dentist

paramedic

plumber

librarian

1. Who helps by fixing leaky pipes? _____

2. Who helps by sharing good books? _____

3. Who helps by fixing light switches? _____

4. Who helps by keeping teeth healthy? _____

5. Who helps by giving people medicine? _____

6. Who helps by taking people to hospitals? _____

To Your Table

How does food get from where it grows to where you eat it? Look at the pictures. They show the order that this happens. Write down what is happening at each step. Copy the words from the Steps Boxes.

Steps Boxes

You take apples home and eat them there.	Apples are put on trucks and taken to a store.	Apples grow on trees in an orchard.	You shop at a store and buy apples there.

Step 1

_____

_____

_____

Step 2

_____

_____

_____

Step 3

_____

_____

_____

Step 4

_____

_____

_____

Who Did What?

Five children played at the park. Use the clues to decide which child played with which of these things:

bike

jump rope

football

slide

sandbox

Clues Box

- Anna jumped up and down, while Mark started up high and went down low.
- Alex rode around, while Eric dug down deep and Emma played catch.

What did each child do?

Anna played with the _____.

Alex played with the _____.

Emma played with the _____.

Eric played with the _____.

Mark played with the_____.

Party Planning

Five friends wanted to throw a party for their friend. They each took a job so that everything would get done. Read the clues. Decide who did what to plan for the party.

Clues

There was a lot of work to do for the party! The friends split up the jobs. Karen bought the decorations, and Julie came up with the games. Tom bought the present, while Kim picked out a card. Ozzy said he would make sure that good songs were playing during the party.

Write the friend's name next to the picture of what they got for the party.

1. Friend: _____

2. Friend: _____

3. Friend: _____

4. Friend: _____

5. Friend: _____

Which Doesn't Belong?

Circle the animal in each row that does not belong. Tell why. The answer could have to do with what kind of animal it is or what it is called. Think hard!

1.

Why it doesn't belong:

2.

Why it doesn't belong:

3.

Why it doesn't belong:

4.

Why it doesn't belong:

5.

Why it doesn't belong:

Which Color?

Mr. Clark wears a different color of shirt each day during the school week. He has blue shirt, a red one, a purple one, a green one, and a yellow one. Use the clues to decide which color he wore on which day.

Clues

He always starts the school week with his purple shirt and ends the week with his blue one. The shirt he wore on Tuesday was the color of a lemon, and Wednesday's shirt was the color of a ripe tomato. Thursday was St. Patrick's Day.

Use markers or colored pencils to show which color of shirt he wore on each day of the school week.

Monday	Tuesday	Wednesday

Thursday	Friday

Description Match

For each problem, look at the picture in the top box. See how the word beside it describes the picture. Then find which word matches the picture in the bottom box in the same way. Fill in the circle next to the correct word.

1. → sleep
   - (A) pink
   - (B) dream
   - (C) sit

2. → paper
   - (A) metal
   - (B) door
   - (C) lock

3. → sour
   - (A) bee
   - (B) sticky
   - (C) sweet

4. → zero
   - (A) legs
   - (B) eight
   - (C) web

5. → meat
   - (A) dairy
   - (B) liquid
   - (C) drink

This Is To That

Analogies compare things. Fill in the correct circle to complete each analogy.

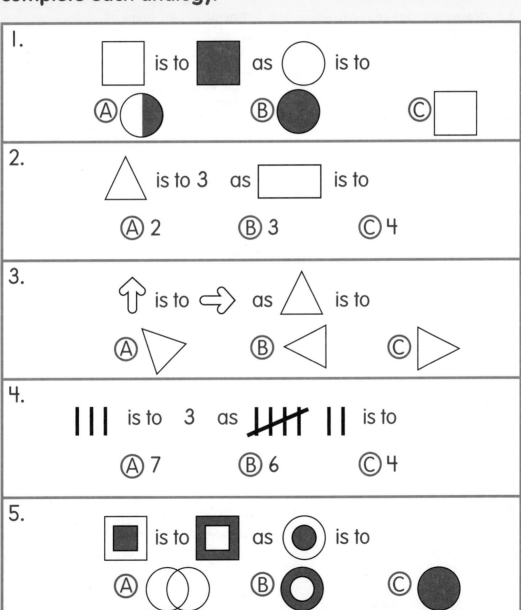

1. ☐ is to ■ as ◯ is to
   - Ⓐ ◖◗ (half-shaded circle)
   - Ⓑ ● (shaded circle)
   - Ⓒ ☐ (square)

2. △ is to 3 as ▭ is to
   - Ⓐ 2
   - Ⓑ 3
   - Ⓒ 4

3. ⬆ is to ➡ as △ is to
   - Ⓐ ▷ (triangle pointing down)
   - Ⓑ ◁ (triangle pointing left)
   - Ⓒ ▷ (triangle pointing right)

4. ||| is to 3 as ⅷ || is to
   - Ⓐ 7
   - Ⓑ 6
   - Ⓒ 4

5. ▣ is to ◻ as ◉ is to
   - Ⓐ ⦾⦿ (two overlapping circles)
   - Ⓑ ◎ (shaded ring)
   - Ⓒ ● (shaded circle)

Answer Key

"Short Matching" (page 6)

a: cat, bag; *e*: pen, bed; *i*: fish, six;
o: dog, mop; *u*: gum, bus; ten, e

"Long Matching" (page 7)

a: train, snake; *e*: tree, cheese; *i*: lime, kite;
o: hose, ghost; *u*: glue, shoe; green, e

"In the Beginning" (page 8)

Row 1: stop, star; *Row 2*: clock, clown;
Row 3: dress, drum; *Row 4*: plane, plant

"At the End" (page 9)

Row 1: fish, brush; Row 2: ant, tent;
Row 3: shell, ball; Row 4: block, duck

"Syllable Sort" (page 10)

1: pear, shark, square, ant; Row 2: apple,
kitten, circle, spider; Row 3: banana,
kangaroo, triangle, butterfly

"Which Are These?" (page 11)

1. ar, 2. ir, 3. or, 4. ar, 5. ur, 6. ir, 7. er, 8. ur,
9. or

"Which Comes First?" (page 12)

1. chicken, 2. car, 3. apple, 4. bug, 5. cake,
6. seven

"Counting Cows" (page 13)

1. 1 cow, 2 cows; 2. 1 duck, 4 ducks;
3. 1 horse, 2 horses; 4. 1 fox, 3 foxes;
5. 2 zebras, 1 zebra

"Out of Order" (page 14)

1. We saw a black cat.
2. The turtle was slow.
3. Is that a blue frog?
4. Her new hat looks great!
5. My cake had six candles.

"Fix 'Em Up!" (page 15)

1. He and I ate candy.
2. Are those shoes blue?
3. That cat is so fast!
4. Will we fly on Friday?
5. We swim a lot in July.

"The Best Word" (page 16)

1. round, 2. warm, 3. smelly, 4. sweet,
5. melting, 6. metal

"Rhyme Time!" (page 17)

1. frog, 2. duck, 3. ants, 4. bug, 5. bird, owl

"A Tree Story" (page 18)

1. 12 (or 14 if counting the two in the title),
2. green and brown, 3. touch, 4. leaves,
5. eggs.

"Best Friends" (page 19)

1. dog; 2. cat; 3. big, smelly, nice, snores;
4. They are both white with black patches
on their faces; 5. the picture

"Finding Information" (page 20)

1. Hearing, 8; 2. Tasting, 18; 3. Touching,
22; 4. Smelling, 13, because the picture
shows a person smelling a flower

"Picture This" (page 21)

Students should draw a unicorn standing
beneath a tree. The unicorn should have a
long tail, a long mane, and a long horn. The
tree should have four apples. The unicorn
should be reaching up to grab an apple in
its mouth.

"All On the Line" (page 22)

1. $14 + 5 = 19$, 2. $13 + 4 = 17$, 3. $9 + 7 = 16$,
4. $17 - 6 = 11$, 5. $11 - 9 = 2$, 6. $13 - 7 = 6$

"Over and Under 100" (page 23)

1. $101 + 9 = 110$, 2. $103 - 8 = 95$,
3. $93 + 8 = 101$, 4. $107 - 16 = 91$,
5. $91 + 10 = 101$, 6. $108 - 12 = 96$

"More or Less" (page 24)

1. $5 < 7$, 2. $9 > 8$, 3. $4 < 5$, 4. $6 > 5$, 5. $<$,
6. $>$, 7. $>$, 8. $=$, 9. $<$, 10. $>$

"Missing Numbers" (page 26)

1. 34; 2. 61; 3. 80; 4. 49; 5. 37; 6. 20; 7. 91;
8. 70; 9. 59; 10. 30; 11. 99; 12. 111; 13. 55,
57; 14. 71, 73; 15. 32, 34; 16. 98, 100

Answer Key

"Skip Ahead" (page 28)

2s: 8, 14, 16, 20; 5s: 15, 25, 30, 45, 50;
10s: 10, 40, 50, 70, 80, 90

"It Adds Up!" (page 29)

1. 37¢, 2. 32¢, 3. 40¢, 4. 75¢, 5. 80¢, 6. 82¢

"Two Problems in One" (page 30)

1. 13 − 7 = 6; 2. 13 + 7 + 8 = 28; 3. 7 − 4 = 3;
4. 4 + 4 + 4 + 4 + 4 + 4 + 4 = 28;
5. 6 + 8 = 14; 6. 20 − 6 − 8 − 4 = 2

"A Colorful Graph" (page 31)

1. green; 2. red and purple; 3. Ms. Mack;
4. 20 (6 + 5 + 4 + 5 = 20); 5. Students
should color 6 bubbles blue, 5 bubbles red,
and 4 bubbles green.

"Living Things" (page 40)

Living: boy, butterfly, tree, dog, bird,
squirrel, flowers, grass; *Non-living*: bench,
drinking fountain, trashcan, park sign, leash

"Parents and Children" (page 41)

1. d; 2. a; 3. c; 4. e; 5. b; least: caterpillar,
tadpole

"Animal Types" (page 42)

mammals: dog, mouse, pig, cow; *reptile*:
crocodile, lizard, snake; *amphibian*: frog,
newt, salamander; *invertebrate*: worm,
spider, fly; big picture: reptile

"The Right Place" (page 43)

1. Place C; 2. Place A; 3. Place B

"Everybody Sleeps!" (page 44)

1. 10 hours; 2. 8 hours; 3. 16 − 8 = 8 hours;
4. We need more sleep when we are younger.

"Everybody Blinks!" (page 45)

1. 60 times; 2. 20 times: 3. C

"Liquid and Solid" (page 46)

1. glass: solid, juice: liquid; 2. oil: liquid, jar:
solid; 3. bowl: solid, water: liquid; fish: solid

"Sunny Planets" (page 47)

1. 3rd; 2. Saturn; 3. Neptune, it is the
farthest from the Sun; 4. Jupiter

"'Tis the Season" (page 48)

summer, winter, spring, fall

"What's the Weather" (page 49)

1. Monday, 2. Wednesday, 3. Thursday,
4. Friday, 5. 5 degrees (80 − 75 = 5),
6. 10 degrees (75 − 65 = 10)

"The Big Four" (page 52)

1. north, south, east, west; 2. south, West;
3. a. south, b. east; 4. a. Hill City, b. Park City

"Getting Around" (page 53)

Accept appropriate responses. Airplane—
airport, train—station, cruise ship—port.

"People Who Help" (page 54)

1. plumber; 2. librarian; 3. electrician;
4. dentist; 5. pharmacist; 6. paramedic

"To Your Table" (page 55)

Step 1: Apples grow on trees in an orchard;
Step 2: Apples are put on trucks and taken
to a store; Step 3: You shop at a store and
buy apples there; Step 4: You take apples
home and eat them there.

"Who Did What?" (page 56)

Anna: jump rope; Alex: bike; Emma:
football; Eric: sandbox; Mark: slide

"Party Planning" (page 57)

1. Tom; 2. Ozzy; 3. Kim; 4. Julie; 5. Karen

"Which Doesn't Belong?" (page 58)

1. whale, not land animal; 2. koala, can't fly;
3. dog, not feline (cat); 4. zebra, no horns;
5. cat, does not end with a "g" (or frog, not
a mammal)

"Which Color?" (page 59)

Monday: purple; Tuesday: yellow;
Wednesday: red; Thursday: green;
Friday: blue

"Description Match" (page 60)

1. C, 2. A, 3. C, 4. B, 5. A

"This Is To That" (page 61)

1. B, 2. C, 3. C, 4. A, 5. B